AF605068

## POETRY BY JAMES HUMPHREY

*THE ATHLETE* (1988) Volume

*AFTER I'M DEAD*
*WILL MY LIFE BEGIN?* (1986) Volume

*IN TRIBUTE TO SURVIVORS* (1984) Chapbook

*IN NEW YORK CITY AIR* (1984) Chapbook

*THE 5¢ POEM* (1981) Chapbook

*THE RE-LEARNING* (1976) Volume

*AN HOMAGE:*
*THE END OF SOME MORE LAND* (1972) Chapbook

*THE VISITOR* (1972) Chapbook

*ARGUMENT FOR LOVE* (1970) Volume

# THE ATHLETE

POEMS BY

JAMES HUMPHREY

POETS ALIVE! PRESS

Charlotte, N.C.

1988

The Athlete

Copyright © 1988 by James Humphrey

All rights reserved. Printed in the United States of America. No part of this book may be used or reproduced in any manner whatsoever without written permission from the publisher except in the case of brief quotations embodied in critical articles and reviews.

For information address Poets Alive! Press, P.O. Box 201, Elizabeth Station, Charlotte, N.C. 28204.

Special thanks to the editors of the following magazines for publishing or accepting for publication some of these poems: *Aileron, Cha Cha Review, The Freedom Voice, New Dog, Now Serving Lunch, The Staten Island Review.*

Many of these poems were read on WGUC-FM, University of Cincinnati, Cincinnati, Ohio, on "Jazz With O.T.", hosted by Oscar Treadwell.

First Printing

LIBRARY OF CONGRESS CATALOGING IN PUBLICATION DATA

Humphrey, James, 1939-
THE ATHLETE

I. Title
PS 3558 U446B73 1988 811'.54 88-78
ISBN 0-936641-16-9 permanent paper(soft cover)

For all the abused children
and adult victims of child abuse

■ ■ ■

# TABLE OF CONTENTS

## I

## II

# THE ATHLETE

# I

*and not a woman in the world*
*to tell it to*

## SHOCK OF JOY!

Small restaurant in a strange city,
ready to begin two days of tests
on my spine at one of the nation's
leading medical centers,

awkwardly adjusting foam cushions
I must lug around and sit on,
as well as one for back.

Unexpected *first* experience,
someone helped! The waitress
—young, good looking!

SHOCK OF JOY!

In a quick second, I felt *me,*
what *I* felt. Not the adult victim
of permanent child abuse, the person
with the diseased spine, the person
who has *never* been told by a woman
what I mean to her.

After that, the usual rushed,
sterile courtesy.

My heart dived into silent rejection,
stepfather laughing, yelling in my head,

YOU'RE WORTHLESS

NOBODY WANTS YOU

YOU'RE WORTHLESS

YOU'RE WORTHLESS

## NOBODY WILL EVER WANT YOU

Able to leave a good tip,
smile, say goodnight to her
—and mean it,
walk out of there;
inside myself, slowly working up
through the scars, there's this guy
who's making another comeback,
even though he doesn't know it.

## THERE I STOOD

*for mother, father and stepfather,*
*who made it all possible*

There I stood
after the tests

alone

in "new-improved" back, chest
and neck braces,

lower back "so badly brutalized
it can't tolerate surgery

—neck, upper and mid-back,
almost as bad
—no surgery there, either

—your spine is that
of an old man

—you're 47, yet
your body, blood and reactions

are of an above-average 25-year-old!"

There I stood

without spirit
or imagination

to rise up to
or fall back on

and not a woman
in the world

to tell it to.

## STREET SURVIVAL

Teen-aged mother going
from cheap hotel to
cheap hotel cleaning rooms,
fucking desperate, failed men
for a meal and sleep

*

Boxer between the
5th and 6th rounds, mouth
full of blood, gurgling
antiseptic, soaked sponge
splattering against swollen
face, heart pounding, mind
full of information, ready
for the round of his life

*

Damp basement below
24-hr cafe, young
apprentice writer sitting
on ketchup cases under
dangling 75-watt bulb
at old typer; first crack
at seeing words beyond pencil

*

Short dumpy girl thrusts
dull religious pamphlets
at everyone, saying in
contemptuous piety "YOU
GOTTA BE SAVED TO SEE HEAVEN!"

*

A boy, a girl in an
abandoned warehouse
trying to beat the

nightmares doing
crack. Colorless
butterflies never to
see the blood-red
flowers making it through
cracked cement as near
as the warehouse's
scourged side nearest
the sunlight

*

Thick black spray can words
on tenement building's
windowless side

BROKEN PROMISES

BROKEN HEARTS

BROKEN BODIES

WATCH OUT!!! DEAD DREAMS

DEAD CHILDREN

DEAD WORLD

# Poetry Readings In A Room With Less Confidence Than The Abandoned Alley Behind The Building

The sexually abused skinny girl
always looking over her shoulder,
face, eyes scared,
who learned too soon
life isn't rewarding.

Middle-aged alcoholic
who can't hit the exact combination
for the poem
he knows will get him on his way.

Jelly-faced woman
who can't look at anyone
because it hurts worse to lose
than it feels good to win.

Young guy imitating Hemingway's
invented masculine virtue,
believing it true.

The girl with cantalope-sized breasts
who writes death sonnets about butterflies.

Heavy-metal couple trying to recapture
in thick, broad brush
visual poems of thunderous guitar licks
and outrageous stage antics.

The guy who missed it, whatever it was,
ending up thinking a hundred-buck bingo win
is all of it.

Their lives orphan, broken without redemption
by fathers, mothers, aunts, uncles.

Alone, rejected in the hard senseless city.
Once a week coming together in this room
trying to soothe the permanent scars.

## while

at age 32
began facing the deep emotional scars
from childhood
trying to learn who I truly am
now I am healing
I'm 48
wanting more than ever
a woman unafraid to commit to love
as the public sidewalk outside this window
cracks wider
while women of all ages walk by
blind
to imagination desire need
to feeling experience's inner truth
afraid to feel love's miracle
while they fill bell-less churches
as one old woman breaks away
willing to take her chances at the secrets
buried deep in her heart
while newlyweds pass waving from dollhouses
while a woman covered with tattoos
runs by yelling
MOTHER GET YOUR CLAWS OUT OF MY CHEST
while a woman on welfare stammers by
obedient futile
while suntanned firm-breasted young women walk by
scrubbed more harmonious than their souls
as limousine doors open for them
while little children sit on the curbing
silent
watching
remembering

# THE ATHLETE

*For Gwen Bell's and Catherine Thompson's*
*Junior and Senior English Students*
*Northeastern High School,*
*Elizabeth City, North Carolina,*
*May 26, 1987*

## I

Since I was 8, all I wanted in life
was to play centerfield for the St. Louis Cardinals.
Stepfather always punished me for doing well.
The better athlete I became, the worse the punishment.
He crippled me.
Ending it in near paralysis when I was 17.

Age 11, I was the only kid in the U.S.
who could drill the ball from the centerfield wall
in a professional park to the plate
on a single, perfect hop, nailing the runner.

That summer, I played midget and junior legion ball.
Some of the guys in legion
were 19 and 20. I started and batted third.
In midgets, I batted fourth. In both leagues,
we were state champions.

Next winter, I started left wing
for the high school hockey team.

First time I broad jumped, I leapt 19 feet 6 inches.
I was 12.
That same spring, I was the fastest 12 to 15-year-old
quarter-miler in the country, with a time of
53 seconds flat.

From age 8 to 12, I boxed in more than 100 fights
mostly against older boys, winning all the matches.

In gym at 16, I ran the mile once
—in tennis shoes
around the football field
in 4 minutes, 10 seconds,
probably a national record.
Nobody checked it out.
In full football gear, I punted the ball
50 yards, lofting it almost as high.

## II

I became a poet
only when it was all that was left me,
except dying,
or giving into paralysis.

I didn't want to become a poet.
I should be wearing a world series
championship ring, be in the hall of fame,
doing color for ABC-TV's Monday Night
Baseball Game of the Week.

At 17, eight months before graduation,
stepfather made me quit highschool.

I lived in bushes and cardboard boxes.
Not expecting to last the winter,
I wrote my first poem *A FALLEN MAN SEARCHING.*
I wanted to define myself
before I starved or froze.

I believed, as I do know,
poems should shatter the surface of reality,
give us a new reality.

But poetry lived in the past, ignored innovation,
human motives, secrets of the heart,
honest emotion, human need,
rewarded those who obeyed its archaic rules,
continued the hollow ritual of snobbery.

### III

I've endured 30 years in a literature
whose bosses
would rather have me out of the way.

I've tried to broaden poetry,
tried to bring itup-to-date
—make it a little ahead of its time
like music and art
—watching it remain the spoiled brat,
the least of literature.
30 years being ignored.

If we don't give it a human, contemporary voice
it will become, like Native Americans,
a lost tribe, confined to isolated areas
speaking entirely to itself.

# SCARS
# A Trilogy

*For My Son Saroyan*

## SCARS I

## THEY WALK BY

### I

They walk by,
tanned, tight bodies
in fine summer dresses.

They walk by,
beautifully scented flesh
covering white, perfect bone.

They walk by,
pretending love,
knowing nothing of

Sensitivity

Risk

Commitment

Courage

Suffering

Pain

Loss

Sacrifice

Imagination

Heart

Spirit

Truth

taking what gives purpose
and dignity to my life
then crushing me,

without even trying.

**II**

Plagued with the deep feeling
I don't
deserve to be loved,

this is the type of woman
I'm attracted to,
fooling myself, thinking

they are special, will
talk to me like
I do count, will give my heart
the tenderness it wants.

**III**

This poem is for
the woman I will never know,
who gives love abundantly

silently holding this page
open a few seconds
after reading it.

## SCARS II

## UNTITLED

### I

Over 20 years with N,
I kept love constant, fresh.
I don't anymore.

I can't feel.

I want out,

but can't leave,
can't earn my own money.

Crippled.

Trapped.

Dependent on a woman
who can't be intimate.

### II

Where did it start?

With mother?

Always emotionless, passive,
mother never gave me love,
simple affection, encouragement,
guidance, discipline, sympathy.

Sometimes she watched stepfather
beat and torture me.

When I begged her to help me,
she would say, "He's not hurting you."

## III

In 1960, when I was 20,
I married for the first time.
D was the same age.
From early childhood through late teens,
was severely abused.

When 11,
her father took her into the woods,
broke into a cabin, forced her
to commit perverse sexual acts
with him and to herself;
chained her naked to a pole
and left her to die.

Found by hunters 4 days later,
she was taken to the hospital,
kept two weeks,
moved to the state orphanage
where she lived until 19.

When we met, I was a delivery boy
for a florist.
D was a receptionist at a city hospital.

We thought we were the first lovers
bound by such deep emotions
words weren't necessary.

## IV

A few days after we were married,
D began going to bed with other men.

In 20 months, she gave birth to
two illegitimate daughters,
the first white, the second black.

The next two years, I raised both babies.

In white America in the early 60's
Black was *not* Beautiful.

I lost an $11,000 a year job
(a lot of money then), moved again
and again, keeping us going as a
two-buck a day janitor,
and stealing from the supermarkets.

1964, D divorced me,
was given custody of both babies,
immediately sent the black one
to the state orphanage.

I haven't seen them since.

**V**

I thought it was my fault.

But D was waiting for
Sir Galahad on the white steed
to carry her off into the sunset
of happiness forever and ever.

She so believed this fantasy real,
the slightest problem threatened her.
Hopping into bed after bed
with man after man,
was getting revenge on her father
for crippling her
—and, keeping Galahad alive.

## VI

Then I met N.

Her angelic face, almost perfect body,
untouched.
Univeristy educated with a solid job
—private secretary to a tv executive.
Strong moral values
—wouldn't date me til after
the divorce was final
—went to mass every morning and Sunday.
Only in church would she let me sit next to her.

I WAS THE LUCKIEST GUY IN THE WORLD!

We were married February 28th, 1966.

I saw it too late.

When we courted, she was quiet
and there weren't problems between us.
About a week into our marriage,
she quit talking all together
and wouldn't discuss ordinary problems.

When I asked what was wrong
or showed I was upset,
she ran away
—five, six, seven times a month
up until Saroyan's birth
ten months later.

Mostly, she was gone overnight,
returning at suppertime, after work.
She wouldn't talk about
why she had left.

Each silent return
was supposed to resolve everything!

With love, with compassion, patience,
in anger,
I tried to explain that leaving so much
and her constant silence were like
small clumps of snow rolling down a mountain,
and the only way to stop them from avalanching
was to talk—say anything,
as long as it was what she felt inside.

I explained lasting love and respect are born
when the defenses are dropped, letting another
person inside, telling them from your guts,
your heart, what you feel,
no matter what it is.

But she only talked when I spoke to her,
was never personal, would never disagree
—never argue, never showed any emotion,
always pleasant.

Our 20th year together,
said she might have been an abused child.

She never saw her parents give each other
affection.
Never heard them speak tenderly.
Never heard them argue.

Never gave her affection,
touched or spoken.

Said she grew up feeling love didn't exist,
feeling she didn't exist.
Would never change.

Still leaves every month or two,
but has never committed adultery
or teased men.

She was a wage earner
all the years we've been married,
which saved me from devouring myself
in the lowest of menial work.

No one can budget better
the little money we have at one time.
And, she's a great cook.

But isn't love more than this?

## VII

Is it I've grown—too late
—or do I now want more
than life can give?

I want a woman not afraid of risk.

A Woman who has stripped away
in herself
her mother's silent,
submissive ways.

A Woman who has accepted as true
her own feelings,
and will intimately talk
about them to me
in her own words.

A Woman who will lead
and control conversation.

A Woman who does not believe
sex is a weapon, sacred
or dirty,
but natural and strengthening.

A Woman who will tell me
what I am to her.

**VIII**

I thought by a life-time of being something
as far away from them as I could be,
I could get away from stepfather and mother.

Do they win after all?

## SCARS III

## RESOLUTION TO BE THE BEST FATHER IN THE WORLD

**I**

During a hot summer sunset
in Sioux City when 8,
I was sitting on an aunt and
uncle's backstep,
getting away from stepfather
inside yelling at mother.

From somewhere in there
came a sudden, loud slam.

At the same moment,
something I had never felt
struck inside me,
deep and hard,
never to leave.

I knew I was going to be
the best father in the world.

The feeling was so strong,
it wouldn't make any difference
how much he beat and tortured me,
or how many times every day
he said I was worthless
and would never amount to anything.

## II

When 11, I pitched midget league baseball,
played centerfield for a junior legion team.
I could rifle the ball from the fence
—350 feet to the plate
a single perfect hop.

During the championship game
(we won!) I made six great catches.
On one, I ran over 100 feet to my right
(the left fielder had tripped and fallen)
and dived to snag a fast-dropping fly
in the torn glove I had found
in the dump.

I felt all through my body
I was a great ballplayer,
deciding flat on my belly,
not only would I be the best father ever
to a house full of kids,
I would be the best centerfielder
the St. Louis Cardinals ever had.

## III

That night stepfather chained me naked
to a small bed,
each wrist handcuffed to the top posts,
ankles cuffed to the bottom posts.

He laid a large butcher knife on my chest,
pointed at my throat.

Throughout the night,
he entered the black room,
laughing horribly,
stuck me with the knife,
drawing blood, and yelled

"THIS IS HOW BAD BOYS ARE TAUGHT
WHEN THEY THINK THEY'RE BETTER
THAN THEIR FATHERS!"

He stuck an ice pick
into my left eye.

I went to the police, principal
and ministers, for help.

No one listened.

No one questioned stepfather.
No one questioned mother.

In the forties and fifties,
kids didn't have rights.
At 17,
I could barely lift my arms.
I could only walk.

**IV**

Saroyan, my son, was born
December 12th, 1966;
my last chance
to be the father I wanted to be.

But still we were living
in a midwest city where
I was labled NIGGER LOVER!
and only allowed menial labor
—the rendering works
—at 75¢ an hour,
so mostly, I worked on raising Saroyan,
who I named after William Saroyan,
while N made the money as a librarian.

**V**

I knew I wouldn't be
a re-enactment of stepfather and mother.
I never doubted I would
be a great father.
Giving love is natural for me.
I feel being given a child

is an honored responsibilty from God,
I accepted happily!

From the beginning,
I gave to Saroyan from my heart,
loved, guided, disciplined him
as my equal,
and when older,
listened to and supported him,
encouraging him to make decisions
in his personal and social
day-to-day life, and to stretch
his imagination and intelligence.

Everyday until he moved
to work full-time and go to college,
I told him I loved him
and hugged him.

I wanted Saroyan to look at the world
in wonder,
yet intuitively know what he wanted,
and when he left home,
be sensitive, responsible, self-sufficient,
capable of taking risks he believed in,
and live from his heart.

## VI

From age 10 to 12,
he drove competitively in quarter midgets,
(similiar to Indy 500 cars,
but one-quarter the size)
receiving the Pepsi National Rookie Driver
of the Year Award,

and was twice given Goodyear Tire Company's
National Driver of the Year Award.

When he graduated from high school,
he received the city's
Outstanding Artist Award and the
O'Henry Writing Award.

At 17, moved to Charlotte, North Carolina,
in his bright red convertible,
rented a house, furnished it,
writing full-time for the weekly newspaper
*Grand National Scene,* the bible of
Winston Cup stock car racing,
and went to college to study
fine art and advertising design.

**VII**

I never once forgot
what I promised myself when I was 8.

I could never play professional baseball,
never to know if I would have
made a difference,
but in the one way left to me

I WAS MAGNIFICENT!

I helped my son be everything
he was capable of being.

## VIII

Maybe stepfather and mother still own me,
but they didn't succeed in dragging me
after them into the hell of their hatred,
and,

MY SON IS FREE!

## For All The Abused Children

Early this morning a guy my age
swinging scissors, long knife,
ran into the local police station
screaming

"I'LL KILL HIM
FOR WHAT HE'S
DONE TO ME!"

not knowing who it was
he wanted to kill.

I know the demon in me
is stepfather, what he wants,
know I'm not responsible
for what he's done to me.

Indelible emotional scars
from when a baby, child, teen,
he's at the center
demanding I obey his evil.

I feel he's always behind me,
watching, ready to attack

I feel I am always doing something bad

I feel I will be punished for everything
good I do

I feel I must do everything in a hurry
before he finds out and takes whatever
I am doing away.

I feel I am being bad when I talk or
write about how I feel.

I feel rejected

I feel deserted

I feel I don't exist

Yet, I live from my heart,
take risks, giving myself completely.

In an age of unrelenting ego
celebrating hypocrisy, possessions,
convenience, mediocrity, alcohol,
drugs, macho narcissim, and violence,

I experience the satisfaction of suffering
and surviving to achieve
that which we all as individuals
deem important.

By grasping life with all I've got,
I'm creating something greater and more moving
than my poems.

# II

*there are times when it's foolish to ask*
*what the cost is keeping the heart alive*

# SAVING MY SANITY

## I

There's no chance for anyone
in this apathetic, isolated
southern town that rejects
goodness and crowns malicious
gossip and ignorance,
though the 19 churches are filled
Sundays, Wednesdays and Fridays.

Girls are cheerless cheerers
who have never felt the magic
of their bodies and emotions.

Boys are empty jocks,
never tasting ragged will,
or dignity.

Parents inarticulate, without
imagination or coherence,
who don't believe anything is real
until seen on tv.

There are no jobs, no hospital, cafe,
movie theatre, art gallery, park,
bar, department store, car wash
or simple skating rink, not even
a bus depot. Gutted buildings
seem bomb-shocked, houses sag.
Layered grime everywhere.

No choices. No excitement
to get the natural juices going.
Nothing on the street for the poet
to absorb.

## II

14 months ago, we fled the city's
cotton mill poverty,
screaming amplified guitars,
about to be kicked out of
rotting tiny rooms
for not making the latest
rent increase.
So bent down, crippled, insanity
the final exit,
nearer than someone
about to speak my first name.

Only decent paying job open,
head of public library
in Gerald, South Carolina.
Norma was hired.

## III

The miracle for me remains
getting out of bed each morning
and getting dressed

trying to get well
without encouragement

believing in a God
who has never gotten involved
in my life

still wanting the raw sources
of joy, of love.

The miracle is I care.

I experience tragedy,
not futility.

I know courage of the heart
is rare.

I have learned to say Beg
with Dignity.

## Maybe I Confuse Them

### I

I have lived here a full two years
and no one has talked to me,
though I have attempted
to strike up many conversations.

Maybe I confuse them.
I'm not like their husbands or wives,
boyfriends or girlfriends, brothers
or sisters, fathers and mothers, or
fundamentalist preachers.
Literal belief in the Bible
is used to suffocate individual inner-growth,
questioning and risk.

Truth doesn't exist,
only an ugly self-preservation.

A few boys and girls who graduate high school
and want to grow,
leave.
Girls who stay become clerks in small
county grocery stores, the five & dime, waitress
in the highway cafes and bars, soon marry
taking orders from little-educated husbands
who try to make it as construction workers
and farm hands, carrying shotguns horizontal
across the back window of their pick-ups.

## II

I'm an outsider, and outsiders aren't welcome.
They say we represent change,
and change isn't wanted.
They want everyone to stay as they are,
dead or dying.

They die so willingly,
not knowing they are dying, without discovering
their true selves, their true existance.

This, not unhappiness, is the tragedy of life.

# Oh, Jim

Desperate for companionship, $72
to my name, I'm off in enduring
Maverick to a southern city
I haven't been to since moving to
Gerald.

First stop, Loop Cafe for breakfast.
Used to give benefit readings here.
I'm not acknowledged.

University library has yet to shelve
*After I'm Dead*, though they've had it
three months! I ask the acquisition head
where it is.

"Oh, sir, all of us haven't had our turn
reading it."

"What do you mean?"

"Why, all the librarians and
professional staff."

"Why don't you buy personal copies?"

"Oh, we never do that, Sir. The books
we like are read before being put on
the shelves."

"I wrote a lot of those poems right here,
just to keep warm."

"We know that, Sir. That's what makes
your book special to us."

In frustration, I throw my arms up.
Leave.

Hard, cold rain needles my face.

The newspaper book reviewer is
out of town, so is the child abuse
clinic director. The pool hall
has burned to the ground. Geoff
is in San Francisco. Benny, Jewel,
Al, Vincent have vanished. The
art gallery is closed.

Duck into a corner grocery for a soda.
Scrawny guy trapped in another kind of
desperation demands my money
from the other side of a double-barreled shotgun.

Give it to him. He, partner
run out back door.

Go to the car, get the ten *After I'm Dead*
I brought along, hawk them in the
affluent part of downtown. Sell four.
Buy gas, head for Gerald.

Somewhere, stop at small cafe for sandwich.
Only other customer, a fat woman and
her two sons about 5 or 6. I want
to bury my head in her enormous breasts,
CRY and CRY and CRY, become a sobbing child
at the breasts of a mother I never had.

# WHATEVER HAPPENED TO TRUSTING YOURSELF

*For Julie*

## I

Three weeks now
an attractive woman about 30
has been walking by my study
10 to 12 times every week day,

sometimes looking at me, smiling.
Several evenings she's parked her car
at the curb. When I go out,
she drives away.

A tease? Shy? What?

The next day I'm in the front yard
when she walks by.
I smile, pleasantly ask
if she can talk for a minute.

Rigid, looking away, voice shrill:
"No. I'm a married woman."

"What's going to happen if we talk?"

"We just can't—I'm married."

"Why do you walk by the front of my house
so often?"

"It's the way I walk."

"Only recently.
Why do you park here in the evening?"

"I don't."

"Sure you do—it's okay."

"I don't do that."

Jaws, lips pulled tighter
embracing the rock
that had become her tongue,
blocking the song
that wanted to be sung.

"Why won't you look at me?"

"People will talk."

"Aw, come on—so what
—small towns always talk
so they don't have to
get involved in what's important."

"I can't be seen with you
—you shouldn't be seen talking to me."

## II

She walks by 10 to 12 times every week day
locked tight in a wasted, trembling muscle
commonly called a heart.

# December 16th, 1986

*For Julie*

## I

Choral excerpts from Handel's *Messiah*
on radio. I'm eating oatmeal in kitchen.
Light knock at door.
Jessie, a commercial fisherman
and my friend, hands me a good-sized
Rock bass.

"Supper," he says smiling,
"Looks like a pretty day
this one's gonna be."

## II

Filled the sink with cold water.
Bass nearly as long, eyes glassy,
laid on its side, not moving
but breathing!

## III

I walk to the post office.
Mail box empty.

Leaving, Julie is walking up the sidewalk!
Our shoulders almost touch!
My heart goes off like a pinball machine!
"Hi, Julie!"

She looks away, looks
at me, a tiny smile there!
"Hi."

More than two years Julie has walked
by my study, and we've seen each other
on the street.
This is the first time she's acknowledged me!

**IV**

She doesn't know my spine might quit
in another year.
I want her to know, but not in passing.
I want to make love with her after I say it.

I want Julie to be the last woman
I make love with before paralysis wins.

**V**

But that first smile and "Hi" are enough
bright sun
to get me on home, fill a bucket with water,
carry the fish to the river,
watch it slowly swim down into the dark water,
and say to the blue sky,
"Yes, this *is* a pretty day!"

# When It's Important Or Essential To Me I'm *Never* Allowed To Have It

*For Julie*

## I

Christmas Eve Day, 1986,
pain huge in spine.
Decide to wash car anyway,
filling buckets of water
from kitchen sink

and play traditional Christmas albums
on front porch, next to car.
Washing it an excuse to feel close to Julie
when she walks by, hoping she'll know
the music is for her.

Bulldozer unexpectedly appears behind
the house to level the ground from the
downed county building,
its thunderous roar at full-throttle,
drowns the carols.

Julie walks by.

I'm kneeling, washing a rear hub-cap.
She doesn't see me
or look at the porch.

## II

The silence of God
throughout the Holocaust.

Was He present?

The silence of God
throughout my life.

Is He present?

Only He can answer,

but He doesn't

as new children are raped,
beaten, tortured, abandoned,
scarred for life,

never experiencing tenderness
from another

as paralysis, my final shame,
waits laughing, almost in sight.

# The Most Beautiful Woman In The World Can Only Give What She Has Inside Of Her

## I

Noon today Julie phoned,
asked me to meet her
—9 p.m., the high school parking lot.
Said she realized her feelings for me
were good.

I believed she would be there.

I go with wonder.

Only empty beer cans,
plastic soft drink containers
and along the edge
shivering dried-up zinnias,
as a V of geese go over
my heart can't hear.

## II

Next day, I phone her
ask why she didn't meet me.

"You know why."

"No I don't."

"Men only want one thing."

"Julie, I'm sorry, truly,
you've been degraded to something you're not."

"Yah—sure—I gotta go."

"I want to be your friend.
Sex doesn't have to be a part of it.
We can talk—just over the phone.
I'm sure you know my health is lousy,
and everyone ignores me.
Maybe we can help eachother."

She hung up.

# THE FINAL JULIE POEM

Julie doesn't walk by anymore.
Like other unimaginative southern women
who follow fundamentalism,
she is controlled by fear and obedience.

Blind faith in dogma
killing natural feelings.

Her absence helped me discover:

because mother never talked to me,
it's natural to be attracted to women
who will abuse me with silence.

Cleansing truth at the center of *I*.

I'm ready for what I've missed
in three-quarters of a lifetime.

Ready for a woman's articulation
and gentleness.

I want my blood mine!

# A Beautiful 16-Year-Old Girl Was In My Study

*For Jennifer*

Three years
these four walls have been guillotine
to my never-answered need:
a woman open with love.

Yesterday, a tired woman and her beautiful daughter
were here to see about renting this house.
The mother wanted to know about heating costs,
insulation, plumbing, wiring, insects.
Her daughter asked if she could have this room
I write in for her bedroom.

These guillotine walls know more of my suffering
than my poems can say,
these same walls forever dumb to the beautiful girl
soon to undress before them, sleep and dream
before them, be happy and sad before them,
and maybe grow inside.

There are times when it's foolish to ask
what the cost is keeping the heart alive.

## No One Understands The Pain Or Suffering Of Another

*For All The Women I Have Known,*
*Afraid Of Their True Heart*

### ONE

No one understands the pain
or suffering of another.
No one knows what is felt
and needs to be expressed,
or tries to know,
or wants to.

Sometimes too weak to lift self
from floor to the bed.
Never a voice near my ear:
sweet flute crushing my screams.

Why do people hide what they feel?
It takes so much time.
The world getting further and further apart
as the nuclear holocaust gets closer and closer.

### TWO
### MOVING

End of September, '87, Norma and I
moved from Gerald to Charlotte,
she to head a public library branch
and me to help find beds for the homeless,
cook and counsel with them.

An unscrupulous landlord rented us a house
near the public housing project.

Whites weren't welcome.

Within a week, our car tires were slashed,
house windows broken, I was purposely struck
by a car as I crossed an intersection,
a trained German Shepherd attacked me from behind.

I quit working with the homeless.
I quit believing God was involved with my life.

## THREE

## HAPPINESS DEPENDS ON DECISIONS, NOT CONDITIONS

18 years since I've seen Kathy.
18 years since I've talked to her.
18 years since I have quietly and gently loved her.

Christmas week '87 paralysis tries to enter me,
total defeat feeding it.
I need to be with her, find strength giving to her.

I phone.
She tells me to come to Chicago.

I drive without braces!

I'm surprised she lives in a condo,
but all too soon nearly broken
at her extreme change.

Constant, urgent, empty TALK TALK TALK
about quick, clever, uncommitted episodes
with power positioned peers
who, like Kathy,
are without a past,without memory,
without a heart.

I had begun with something real.
There was cleansing in that.
There was strength.

Maybe suffering is a special love from God.

## FOUR
## MY LAST HURRAH

It was necessary to return to Iowa,
my birthplace,
let all the stress, pain and suffering drain
down through my feet
into the rich humus soil
I was born from.

Driving into Northeastern Iowa's farm country,
winter's first blizzard rushing in from Canada.
An Amish farmer let me stay in a barn.
In the dark loft of loose, fresh hay, wrapped
in my sleeping bag listening to the wind gain force
as it drifted snow in layers around the barn
like overflowing whipped cream,
all of the rich love for Kathy still abundant
in the depths of my deep commitment to life
left silent,
as though it never existed.

I tried to cry. Couldn't.

In the morning, a 12-year-old boy brought me
home-made bread, raspberry jam, hot cereal
and fresh warm milk.

"Do you want to continue with the land
when it's your turn?" I ask.

He nods humbly and asks, "What is your work?"

"I play centerfield for the St. Louis Cardinals."

His face puzzles.

I smile, saying, "They're a professional baseball team."

"Yes, I have heard of baseball, but not
of Saints playing it."

"I'll explain while helping you do chores, okay?"

He nods, says the livestock should be fed.

## FIVE

## WOMEN, I EXPECTED MORE FROM YOU!

Women, I expected more from you!
Don't come to my grave sobbing, bearing roses!
Don't come to my grave at all!

Guilt
Apology
Remorse
Shame

easy to absolve.

Maybe my deep sadness for you

will end when my flesh is dust.

But will my bones weep?

Charlotte, North Carolina
January 2nd-25th, 1988

JAMES HUMPHREY was born in Sioux City, Iowa, February 20th, 1939. From age 5 to 16, he was forced to live with a sadistic stepfather and passive mother. They lived in poverty, often moving throughout the Midwest. Big enough physically at 16, he beat up the six-foot stepfather and left, never to return.

Not having a guardian, he wasn't allowed to continue high school. The next winter, in poor health, living in Iowa in bushes and cardboard boxes, not expecting to last until spring, he wrote his first poem, *A Fallen Man Searching*, which appeared unchanged in his chapbook *In Tribute To Survivors* (1984).

The constant physical, mental and emotional abuse beaten and tortured into him when a child and young teen, the severe circumstances *and* reason for writing his first poem: "The intention was to define myself in a single piece before starving or freezing to death," set the foundation for the raw emotions he bravely enters in his daily living and daring simplicity when he writes.

With the maturing of his writing, to say his poems are direct, honest and personal is secondary. Without trying to do so, he has set a new standard in American poetry long overdue: to discover your heart, open it, and live from it with all your might.

At age 34 he became a college student for the first time

SAROYAN HUMPHREY

entering Brown University, graduating with distinction two-and-a-half years later with an MA in Creative Writing.

For the last seven years he has lived in the South where all of these poems were written. Living in Charlotte, North Carolina, since September 1987, his wife Norma is the Scaleybark Branch Librarian. Their son Saroyan (named after William) has been on his own since graduating from high school in 1984. He lives in Charlotte and graduated from college in winter '87 with a degree in Commercial Art/Design. He is Art Director for *Grand National Illustrated*, a bi-monthly magazine with international distribution covering Winston Cup Grand National stock car racing.

■ ■ ■